read the signals
the body language handbook

Crabtree Publishing Company

www.crabtreebooks.com

Crabtree Publishing Company
www.crabtreebooks.com

Author: Dr. Melissa Sayer
Editor: Molly Aloian
Proofreader: Adrianna Morganelli
Project coordinator: Robert Walker
Production coordinator: Margaret Amy Salter
Prepress technician: Margaret Amy Salter
Project editor: Victoria Garrard
Project designer: Sara Greasley

Every effort has been made to trace copyright holders, and we apologize in advance for any omissions. We would be pleased to insert the appropriate acknowledgments in any subsequent edition of this publication.

Picture credits:

iStockphoto: p. 6, 32

Sara Greasley and Hayley Terry: front cover (bottom), back cover (bottom), p. 9 (center right), 11, 13, 15, 16, 21 (bottom), 23 (bottom), 25, 26, 28, 31, 33, 37 (bottom), 38, 40

Peter Brooker/Rex Features: p. 35 (top)

Shutterstock: p. 1, 2, 4, 5, 7, 8, 9 (top), 10, 12, 14, 17, 19 (top), 19 (bottom), 20, 21 (top), 22, 23 (top), 24, 27, 29, 30, 35 (bottom), 36, 37 (center right), 39, 41, 42, 43, 44

Ticktock Media Archive: front cover (top), back cover (top)

Library and Archives Canada Cataloguing in Publication

Naik, Anita
     Read the signals : the body language handbook / Anita Naik.

(Really useful handbooks)
Includes index.
ISBN 978-0-7787-4388-0 (bound).--ISBN 978-0-7787-4401-6 (pbk.)

     1. Body language--Juvenile literature. I. Title. II. Series: Really useful handbooks

BF637.N66N33 2009   j153.6'9   C2008-907871-3

Library of Congress Cataloging-in-Publication Data

Naik, Anita.
    Read the signals : the body language handbook / Anita Naik.
       p. cm. -- (Really useful handbooks)
    Includes index.
    ISBN 978-0-7787-4401-6 (pbk. : alk. paper) -- ISBN 978-0-7787-4388-0 (reinforced library binding : alk. paper)
    1. Body language--Juvenile literature. I. Title. II. Series.

BF637.N66N34 2009
153.6'9--dc22

2008052358

Crabtree Publishing Company
www.crabtreebooks.com   1-800-387-7650

Published in Canada
Crabtree Publishing
616 Welland Ave.
St. Catharines, Ontario
L2M 5V6

Published in the United States
Crabtree Publishing
PMB16A
350 Fifth Ave., Suite 3308
New York, NY 10118

contents

chapter 1: body language

chapter 2: flirting

chapter 3: communication

chapter 4: be confident

introduction

Can someone really tell what I'm like just by looking at me?

Body language gives away more than you think. If you want to improve the impression you make, change the way people respond to you, and even get new people to like you, you need to look at improving your **body language**.

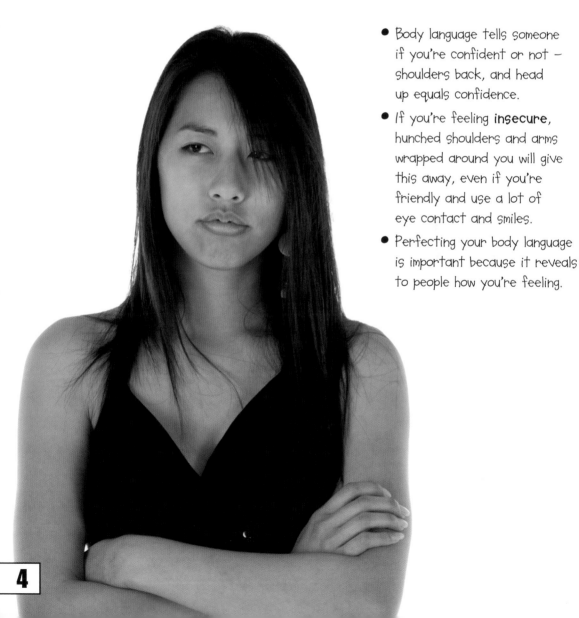

- Body language tells someone if you're confident or not — shoulders back, and head up equals confidence.

- If you're feeling **insecure**, hunched shoulders and arms wrapped around you will give this away, even if you're friendly and use a lot of eye contact and smiles.

- Perfecting your body language is important because it reveals to people how you're feeling.

How can I make a positive impact with my body language?

Start by correcting your **posture**. How you hold your body tells others a lot about how confident and assured you are. If you want to portray openness and friendliness:

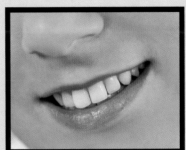

• pull in your stomach
• roll your shoulders back
• deflate your chest
• keep your head up
• put a smile on your face.

This immediately tells others you're an outgoing person and someone they'd love to know.

Did you know?

When it comes to communicating with others, 55% comes from your body language, 38% from the tone of your voice and only 7% from what you actually say.

Body language tips

How to tell if:	What they will do:
Someone is nervous	Fidgeting and/or playing with hair
Someone is feeling unconfident	A puffed up chest
Someone is being fake	A smile that doesn't reach his or her eyes
Someone is attracted to you	A sideways glance and smile
Someone is disinterested	They glance beyond you while talking
Someone is lying	They rub their nose while speaking
Someone likes you	They touch your arm when speaking to you

making an entrance

No one ever notices me – what can I do?

You need to get people to notice you for the right reasons. Here's how to do it.

- Think about the people you notice and consider what it is that makes them stand out.

- The chances are it's not what they are doing to get attention, but how they appear to others. This doesn't mean you have to morph into your school's inner clique, just make the most of who you are!

- Emphasize your good points so that you feel confident. For example, show off your great smile.

- Then, hold yourself confidently because when it comes to standing out from the crowd, it's all about confidence and boldness.

How can I walk into a room with confidence?

- Believe you are just as worthy as everyone else: otherwise you'll literally feel yourself shrinking as you step over the threshold.
- Focus on your posture: head up, big smile, and walk in.
- Linger in the doorway for a second to "people spot."
- Head for your best friend or nearest friendly person.

How to make the wrong entrance

- Wear something risqué
- Be over the top and embarrassing
- Shout, "I'M HERE!"
- Walk too fast
- Get drunk before you walk in

Did you know?

When we're nervous, the muscles in our faces make us look tense and unfriendly. To loosen up, wiggle your jaw from side to side and raise and lower your eyebrows. This will relax your face, release tension, and help you to exude calmness.

be popular

How can I get others to like me?

The secret to being popular is easier than you think.

- People like people who can be bothered to remember facts about them.
  Try to remember people's names and at least two other facts about them.

- Just knowing these things will make them feel liked
  by you and will make them more open to you.

- At the same time be interested and interesting as this is
  a signal to others that you're not self-obsessed or strange.

I can be quite emotional and friends say this puts new people off. Is that true?

- Being over emotional can put off prospective friends. While it's essential to be yourself, make sure you're not being too over the top about it.
- Big displays of anger, loud laughing, or even crying can make people step back when they don't know you.
- Constant whining, being depressing and acting negative do the same.
- If you're trying to impress someone, put your best foot forward ... but in a more laid back way.

How to tell if someone wants to be friends

- They smile when they see you.
- They go out of their way to say hello.
- They offer to help you with something.
- They compliment you.
- They're sincere with you.
- You get a gut feeling they like you.

Did you know?

Mirroring someone's body language (in a subtle way) puts them at ease and makes them feel more comfortable around you.

How to put people off

- Be aggressive
- Be bullying
- Tell others what to think
- Be pushy
- Insist you are friends

9

how to spot a fake

I can never spot if someone is being fake with me. How can I tell if someone is lying?

It pays in life to be able to spot the liars, fakes, and cheats and you don't have to be a mind reader to do it.

- The smile is the facial feature that we all use the most and it's the one most fake people use when trying to cover up their insincerity.

- You can spot a fake smile by observing how real smiles work. Honest smiles involve all our facial muscles and reach up close to the eyes. Fake ones don't (try both a fake and real one in a mirror).

- Fake smiles are also held too long and disappear right away, while real ones fade gradually.

I've heard fidgeting is a sign of lying. Is this true?

- While fidgeting can be a sign of lying it can also be a sign that you're naturally jumpy or that you have an itch.
- Experts suggest if you want to "read" someone properly you should look for a **cluster of signals** all happening at once.
- For example fidgeting, a fake smile, nose rubbing, and lack of eye contact would suggest something was amiss.
- Also, people who are lying are often very specific whereas those telling the truth admit to not remembering all the details.

How to spot a liar

1) They give you vague information when you ask for an explanation.
2) They won't look you in the eye or won't stop looking in your eyes (normal people glance and then glance away when speaking).
3) They try to change the subject.
4) They speak slowly (compared to their usual way of speaking).

Did you know?

When someone lies, chemicals are released from the brain. This makes the nose itch and causes the liar to rub or scratch his or her nose.

flirting with confidence

I am a useless flirt! How can I get someone's attention?

- **Flirting** is about having great body language.
- It's a way to charm someone, let them know you like them, and best of all, improve your own confidence and have some fun.
- The best flirting tip is to realize that flirting is not about how clever or beautiful you are, but about the signals you send out.
- To get it right, imagine the nicest thing someone ever said to you and let that thought reach your lips. This will give you a mega-watt smile that you can follow up with the ultimate flirt tip...

How can I get the courage to flirt?

To find the courage to take a risk, ask yourself – what have I got to lose? The chances are you have more to lose by not taking a risk, i.e. are you going to sit back and wait for people to come to you all your life?

The ultimate flirt tip

1) Look at someone you like until they look back at you and then hold their gaze for a second.

2) Look away and within a second look back and smile at them.

3) If they smile back, you've got them hooked! Now go over and talk to them.

Flirting dos and don'ts

DO practice to get better
DO be yourself
DON'T flirt with with inappropriate people, such as your teacher or boss

Remember

When flirting, don't go into oversell. Less if often more.

flirtatious body language

How can I tell if someone is flirting with me?

Recognizing someone's body language is key when it comes to flirting as it will stop you from approaching someone who's not interested, or rejecting someone who is.

If you can't tell by what someone is saying, look for the following body language:

- Are they mirroring your body language?
- Are they lightly touching your arm or leg when they speak?
- Have they moved in closer than a friend would?
- Are they telling you something personal?
- All of the above are signs that they like you. They are literally trying to get closer to you by telling you something intimate and/or moving closer. They are trying to get you to like them by mirroring your body language. And they are showing you they appreciate you by touching you.

I'm not the touchy feely type—what should I do?

If you're not keen on flirting with your body (what is known as **tactile communication**) the trick is to make your face do the work. Research shows that women who express interest and energy through lively facial expressions attract more men. The key is not to pull a series of silly exaggerated faces but keep your expressions energetic and full of life. Practice in front of a mirror.

Did you know?

The closer two people are emotionally, the more similar their body language.

Signs someone's interested in you

- They ask you about yourself.
- They remember things about you.
- They look interested when you say something.
- They give you compliments.
- They don't ignore you when their friends appear.

- They call when they say they will.
- They treat you well.
- They smile when they see you.
- They are interested in your life.
- They like you for who you are.

how to attract someone you like

There's someone I like, but I don't know how to act when they're around. How can I get them to like me?

- Playing mind games, faking who you are, and pretending to not like them when you do only works in the movies.

- To find a partner in real life, you need to show them the real you, so:

1 Be interested

2 Flirt

3 Talk to them

4 Smile a lot

- You can't do more than that. If that doesn't work, either they're with someone already, or they're just not your type. If this happens, try not to feel rejected and just move on.

Do first impressions count?

- First impressions are everything ... but it's not down to how you look. People make up their mind about you from your attitude and behavior, for example how much you smile.
- So if you like someone and want to show it, act relaxed but be interested.
- Playing hard to get is a myth. If you act like you're bored and don't care, the first impression you're giving is that you're really not interested.

What not to do

- Take on his or her interests.
- Try to be like their ex.
- Pretend to be something you're not.
- Flirt with their friends.
- Play hard to get.
- Treat them mean (it won't keep them keen).
- Ignore them when you see them.

Did you know?

Don't worry if someone you like doesn't chat as much as you. Studies show women talk almost three times as much as men, with the average woman chalking up 20,000 words in a day – 13,000 more than the average man.

how to tell if someone likes you

I never seem to notice the obvious when I am at parties. Recently I shut someone down who was really into me. Help!

It's easy to miss obvious signals that someone likes you.
Here's how to tell if the object of your affection likes you or not.

- The trick is to look for clusters of signals. So, if someone smiles at you, comes over to talk to you, goes out of their way to make you laugh, and comes in close when you speak, the chances are they really like you.

- If they then do something known as reciprocal disclosure – trade a personal piece of information with you such as telling you something others don't know – they really, really like you.

- Finally, if they make a vague suggestion of meeting up or doing something, they're not just throwing the idea out there. They're telling you they want to see you again, but want you to say yes by giving them your number.

My friends say a guy I like likes me back because he is rude when I speak to him. Are they right?

People have a lot of theories on how to tell if someone likes another person. However, the "treat them mean to keep them keen" theory is wrong. Even the shyest person in the world wouldn't be rude to someone he really likes. Sorry but your friends are wrong.

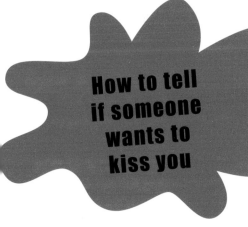

How to tell if someone wants to kiss you

1) They'll come in close to you to see if you're responsive to them. If you're not, your instant knee jerk reaction will be to pull your body back without even thinking about it.

2) They might gently lick their lips in preparation for a kiss (a small involuntary movement).

3) They might briefly touch your hair, or stroke your cheek. These are more personal body areas than your arm, and are a good way to gauge if someone wants to kiss you back.

19

speaking with confidence

How can I make my voice sound more confident?

To be a social hit you don't have to be the cleverest or the funniest person around, you just need work on perfecting a confident pitch of voice or **vocal tone**. Remember to:

- Stand or sit up straight so your voice isn't squashed somewhere inside you!

- Take a couple of deep breaths and try to make your voice come from your diaphragm/abdomen rather than your throat. To locate the right place, try humming and feeling it in your stomach.

- Talking from this place immediately slows your voice down. Fast talking is a sign of nervousness so speaking slowly helps you to sound confident and appealing.

How can I learn to speak so people listen?

Think about what you're saying. Confident speakers express opinions, and ask questions, but more importantly they listen to others, and don't feel they have to talk all the time.

Quick Quiz

Are you a confident speaker?

A friend's mom asks you what you think about the book you're reading, do you:

a) Look at your friends to see what they think.

b) Say, "I don't know."

c) Say what you think she wants to hear.

d) Say you liked a certain part.

Answer a – Your need to fit in stops you from speaking with confidence.

Answer b – Your **shyness** stops you from believing your opinions are valid.

Answer c – Your need for approval makes you censor what you say.

Answer d – You're not afraid to say what you think.

Speaking without confidence

1) You answer every question with a question.

2) You let your sentences go up at the end, a sign to someone that you're unsure of yourself.

3) You cover your mouth when you speak.

making new friends

We're moving towns and I'm not sure how to make new friends.

There is an art to making friends and it all starts with being yourself. Easier said than done, but the key is to show them that you're interested in them, so:

- Ask them questions about themselves – what's your name, what do you do on weekends, who do you know?

- Share something personal with them. This is known as reciprocal disclosure and is a way of letting others know you want to be friends. Not too personal though – you don't want to make people uncomfortable. For example, it's fine to tell someone you had your heart broken but don't go into the gory details.

- Tell them a funny story – humor goes a long way when it comes to cementing new friendships.

Where to find new friends

- Through other friends
- By talking to someone you like the look of, no matter where you are
- Through hobbies and clubs
- Through siblings

How not to make new friends

- Lie to people about who you are.
- Be who you think they want you to be.
- Gossip behind their backs.
- Use them to get what you want.

talking to people you don't know

I find it really hard to talk to people I don't know at parties or at new places. What should I do?

Do you feel yourself on the outside looking in when you're out with new people or at a party? If so, here's how to make conversation in any social situation.

- It may sound silly, but when you're all alone in your room, read your favorite book out loud so that you can get used to the sound of your voice.

- Make a pact to talk to one new person every day whether it's to say hello to a shop assistant or make a comment to someone when you're waiting in line.

- Talking to people you're never going to meet again is liberating and will give you confidence to start conversations with people when you're at parties or in new places.

I feel really self-conscious when I talk to new people. Help!

To zap self-consciousness, project outward instead of inward. Instead of thinking, "What does this person think of me? Do they like me? Am I boring them?" think about what you're saying to them, what they are saying back to you, and above all, what's happening around you.

Top talking tips

1) Smile – it attracts people to you.

2) Ask questions – it makes people feel comfortable.

3) Talk about something everyone can join in with like TV or music.

4) Don't rush to fill silences.

5) Don't be afraid to say you find it hard to talk to new people.

6) Don't gossip about people, you never know who knows who.

7) If you want to approach someone at a party, stop thinking and start doing. Jump in and say hello! Chances are you want to speak to them because they have already sent you friendly signs via their body language.

8) If you're in a scary nerve–wracking social situation, all you have to do is say, "Hello – are you a friend of X?" Then let the conversation flow from there.

the art of conversation

Small talk is crucial in social situations. Know how to do it right and you'll always have a good time.

- If all the usual suspects don't work (TV, films, music, food), try gauging what the person you're with is into.
- Look at his/her clothes and compliment something they have on.
- Better still, talk about something you've read in a paper or heard on the radio, or make them laugh by recounting a funny anecdote.
- All of these things instantly put people at ease and get them to open up.

What shouldn't I say?

Depressing, negative, and gloomy subjects don't go down well as small talk, and neither does malicious gossip. Inappropriate jokes are also a no-no, as are strong opinions that could offend. If you're unsure, consider what topics you'd hate a stranger to talk to you about and steer clear of those.

??!!

Top five conversation stoppers

1) Don't you think X is ugly/smelly?

2) My cat just died

3) I think I have a contagious disease

4) I feel like crying

5) Didn't you cheat on my sister?

Did you know?

If you let people talk about themselves three times more than you talk about yourself, you're going to be super popular at a party.

Eight steps to small talk at a party

1) Introduce yourself by making a connection to the party host – "Hi, I'm X, a friend of X."

2) Ask a person their name and use it at least once when talking to them.

3) Look for connections you can talk about.

4) If there are no connections, compliment the person.

5) Tell them something about you. Make it funny and interesting, but not strange.

6) Listen to what they say to you and ask them another question off the back of their comment.

7) If conversation flows, suggest swapping emails.

8) Keep everything light and easy – it's small talk after all!

talking to authority figures

People don't take me seriously when I talk to them. What should I do?

It can be scary and difficult, but talking to people in authority and getting your way isn't impossible.

- Know your argument inside out. Be clear about what you want, why you want it, and show them how you intend to achieve it.
- Stay calm and reasonable when you speak. It's easy for things to get heated and out of control, especially with parents, so stay focused.
- Use confident body language: sit up straight, use eye contact, and keep your tone of voice even.
- Be willing to compromise. It may not be what you want, but it shows them you're mature enough to settle for the middle ground.

I'm nervous around my teacher. How do I talk to her?

Many people get nervous around authority figures and it can be especially hard when a teacher is unapproachable. Remember, their job is to help you and so you are entitled to talk to them if you have a problem. If you're nervous, be clear, be concise, and know what you want from them. For example, you might find their subject hard and want help, so:

1) Tell them exactly what's wrong
2) Keep it short and to the point (don't point a finger of blame)
3) Tell them what you need from them, more help in class or more direction.

Remember

- Use positive language.
- Remind yourself that your point is as valid as theirs.
- Use confident body language.
- If you lose your voice, breathe out – it immediately calms you down.

Negotiation tips

- Work out what you need to say and what you want before you talk to someone.
- Negotiate by showing them you're willing to compromise if they are.
- Make sure you're being assertive (using positive language and actions) and not aggressive (using angry words and actions).

straight talking

Being a straight talker is difficult, and if you find it hard to stand up for yourself, you're not alone. However hard things sometimes need to be said.

My friend is always borrowing my stuff without asking. I want to tell her to stop – how do I do it?

Try to be fair when you say tough things. Friends are not mind readers and don't always know they are bugging you if you haven't told them before. The trick is to stay calm, be firm, and be clear but also reassuring. In this case:

1) Tell her she's a great friend but all this borrowing is getting you down.
2) Explain you don't want her to do it any more but follow up with a compromise. For example in an emergency she can borrow from you.
3) Finally, ask her if she understands. This last bit is important because in hearing a friend's version of what you have just said, you can work out if they have misunderstood you or not.

Remember

- Treat friends the way you expect to be treated. Hearing hard things is hurtful even if it needs to be said.
- Accept an apology and get over it. Going on and on about something is what kills friendships.
- Make sure you say what you want a person to do to make amends.
- Stand your ground even if the other person gets emotional.
- Walk away if things get angry.
- Don't feel guilty.
- Don't apologize (unless of course you've got it wrong).

Celebrity tough talkers

"If I make a fool of myself, who cares? I'm not frightened by anyone's perception of me."

Angelina Jolie, actress known for speaking her mind about everything from body issues to world politics.

"I think you have to judge everything based on your personal taste. And if that means being critical, so be it."

Simon Cowell, American Idol and X Factor judge, known for telling it like it is.

"I'm tough, ambitious, and I know exactly what I want."

Madonna, singer, actress, and icon

overcoming shyness

Shyness is when feelings of anxiety and discomfort spoil social situations. As painful as it is, you can get over it.

Why is it so bad to be shy?

- The downside of being shy is that it can stop you doing things. For example you don't go for a job because you're too afraid of the interview. Or, you don't answer a question in class because you don't want people to laugh at you.

- Shyness can even stop you making friends and dating because of the fear of embarrassment.

- If you find that your shyness is keeping you from doing stuff, try to put your worries in perspective: making new friends isn't a dangerous situation — even if that's what your brain is telling you.

- Don't shine a spotlight on yourself. Stop worrying about what people think of you and start thinking about what you think of them.

Confidence booster

Shyness affects around 40% of people so you're not alone.

Are all shy people nice?

Shyness is not who you are, but about how you behave. It doesn't mean you're nicer, more horrible, or secretly wiser than anyone else.

Four Ways to Get Over Being Shy

1) Don't imagine everyone is looking at you – they're not. They're too busy looking at themselves!

2) Let go of past experiences – it's what you do right now that counts.

3) Don't take offence. A negative response from someone you don't know is about them, not you and the chances are they are having a bad day.

4) Challenge yourself. The saddest part about shyness is the opportunities you miss because you're too shy to try new things.

It happened to me!

"The way I got over my shyness was to fake confidence. I was always the one waiting for someone to talk to me so I tried smiling more and said hello to people I didn't know. I always made sure I had three questions in my head that I could ask them so there wasn't a weird silence. It really works."

Cassie, 14

how to be outgoing (when you're not)

I am an introvert and find it hard to make myself go out and do things.

- The secret in projecting confidence lies in faking it to make it.
- If you want to be more outgoing, you have to challenge yourself to move out of your comfort zone (the place where you literally feel in control and comfortable.)

- Start small. If you rarely speak up in a group start making your voice heard, and if you never say yes to new things make yourself try something new every day.
- Bear in mind it will feel uncomfortable at first but the stress will recede and your confidence will rise.

Confidence booster

Pretend you're braver than you are. In the comfort of your own room, think of the most confident person you know (or model yourself on a famous person), take a deep breath, and act the way they would for five minutes.

From introvert to extrovert – Model Sophie Dahl

Sophie Dahl's childhood involved being pushed between LA and an English boarding school. This contributed to her depression, shyness and anorexia, all of which she overcame to become a modeling sensation at 18. She later followed in her grandfather Roald's footsteps and became a successful writer.

I want to be more outgoing but my friends keep telling me I'm not like that.

- As much as we love our friends and family, they can unwittingly stop us from becoming the people we want to be.
- While this doesn't mean dump everyone you know, it does mean you need to stretch your social wings so you can meet new people who don't have any prejudged ideas about you.
- This then allows you space to grow and become who you want to be while slowly convincing your old friends it's for the better.

how to be confident in class

How can I show my teacher that I am confident and interested without being teacher's pet?

Contrary to popular belief, loud, obnoxious behavior in class doesn't scream confidence to your teachers and fellow students. Here's what does:

- There are lots of ways to project confidence and thankfully sucking up to a teacher isn't one of them.

- The best way to do it is to be proactive and ask questions. This means speak up if you don't understand something, at least 50% of your class will be with you.

- Ask questions if an explanation leaves you confused and try to clarify what you've heard if you're unsure. Aside from helping your friends, it shows a teacher you're willing and eager to learn.

I'm too scared to answer questions

Speaking up in class is a tough one, especially if you're shy and worried about negative feedback from classmates. Here are some tips:

- Remember it doesn't matter if what you say is wrong.
- Don't wait until you have the right answer, it's a waste of time. The way we learn is by asking and answering and to do this we have to take a risk and speak up.
- The first time you put your hand up is always the hardest. But if you do it, you'll find that it's never as scary or frightening as you think. It gets easier and easier!

Star pupils

1) Natalie Portman (right) – graduated from Harvard with a degree in psychology. As well as being bilingual in Hebrew and English, Portman has studied French, Japanese, German, and Arabic.

2) Jodie Foster – Valedictorian: Le Lycee Francais; magna cum laude grad of Yale; received honorary Doctorate from Yale.

3) Pop divas Madonna and Shakira have an IQ of 140 (between 90 and 110 is normal, over 120 is superior).

Did you know?

Research shows that teachers rate students who are more verbal in class as being more intelligent than those who stay quiet.

getting your way

My friends are good at manipulating me. How can I work on getting my way for a change?

- Getting your way is all about knowing what you want and why.
- Get to grips with those two things and the rest is easy.
- Contrary to popular belief, getting your way is not about being controlling or manipulative. It's about being able to stand up for what you want.
- Step one is wiping the "welcome" sign off your forehead and not allowing everyone to walk all over you.
- Friends will respect you more if you have some boundaries with them. This means being clear about what you do and don't want to do and then being brave enough to say so — no matter how much they try to plead, beg, or bribe you to change your mind.

I'm a real people pleaser – how do I stop?

- You have to stop basing your self-worth on what you do for other people.
- It's good to help others, but not if you're only doing it because you feel it's the only way they'll ever like you.
- To increase your self-esteem and improve your friendships, think about what you want, balance it up with the needs of others and then make your decision.

How to deal with an argumentative person

1) Stay calm. Argumentative people try to dominate conversations by setting the tone and trying to drag you to their level.

2) Keep your body language non-confrontational. That means stay relaxed, don't tighten your neck and shoulders, and don't puff out your chest. This neutralizes someone trying to argue.

3) Walk away if they won't agree to disagree.
If they want to argue, let them argue with themselves!

How to get your way

- Practice asking for small things first.
- Be assertive, not aggressive.
- Be logical with your reasoning.
- Remember no one can read your mind so tell people what you want.
- Watch how others do it.

how to do well in an interview

I've never had an interview before – what do I need to do?

How you project yourself establishes how others judge you, which is why it's essential to get it right in an interview. Think of an interview like an exam and come prepared:

- Know what's expected of you.
- Find out what you need to wear.
- Rehearse what you need to talk about.
- Don't be afraid to research all of this before your scheduled date. Most jobs and schools will tell you what's expected of you in an interview.
- Knowing these facts can alleviate a lot of interview anxiety and enable you to walk in bursting with confidence. This will give you an improved chance of success.

How do I make a good first impression in an interview?

To appear confident, you have to display confident behavior. If you're meeting someone for the first time:

- Walk confidently into the room with a purposeful stride.
- Look your interviewer in the eye and say hello.
- Offer them your hand to shake. It can help to practice this on friends if you're unused to shaking hands. Ensure your handshake exerts a similar pressure to that of the other person. You don't have to worry about letting go, the other person will signal that.
- Then sit down. Keep your posture strong and try not to fidget as this signals anxiety.

Image is everything in an interview

- Come dressed for the part. You'll need to be smart and clean.
- Don't bring too many bags. If you're loaded down ask to leave stuff in reception.
- If you're a flamboyant dresser, try and tone it down.
- Think about what you want your image to say about you and act accordingly.

how to cope with bullying

Bullying is when someone picks on you, threatens you physically, verbally, and/or emotionally and makes your life miserable. If you're being bullied, here are the skills you need to overcome it.

How can I stand up to bullies?

The best way is to tell an adult who can help with what's happening to you.

- It's no good suffering alone, turning the other cheek and/or confronting them.

- Bullies won't realize what you're doing, and so will just continue their campaign of nastiness.

- Telling someone is the bravest and most assertive thing to do.

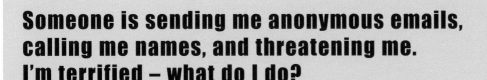

Someone is sending me anonymous emails, calling me names, and threatening me. I'm terrified – what do I do?

- Whether it's face-to-face, online, via cell phones or through emails, it's still bullying! You need to tell someone who can do something about it.
- Start with your parents. They can help you to start tracking down the culprits – it's easier to do than the bullies think.
- Next sign off and don't view your emails until it's sorted out. This way you won't live in fear of what's going to arrive in your mailbox.

What to do if you're being bullied

- Ignore a face-to-face threat. Don't respond, just walk away
- Be assertive and tell someone who can help with what's happening – a teacher, a parent, a relative, or call a helpline for advice
- If you're scared, stay in a group for protection

Who can help you?

- Your parents
- Your teachers/your school
- Relatives
- The Police
- Online bullying websites

Famous people who were bullied and overcame it

Tyra Banks, Steven Spielberg, Ben Stiller, Christina Aguilera, Orlando Bloom and ... Rihanna who was bullied at school for being "white."

- Rihanna was taunted growing up on the Caribbean island of Barbados because she was fair-skinned.
- The 19-year-old, who has a black mother from Guyana and a mixed-race father, says "People would look at me and would curse me out for being light. I didn't understand why."

the social etiquette quiz

When it comes to making it big in a social situation, it's often down to how you handle social etiquette. In other words knowing what's acceptable behavior and what's not.

1. **When you're talking to someone you like, do you:**
a) Keep your eyes solely focused on them and don't even blink?
b) Avoid all eye contact with them as it's embarrassing?
c) Glance at them and then glance away?

2. **On a date would you:**
a) Text message your friends freely?
b) Turn your cell phone off?
c) Secretly call your friends from the toilet?

3. **At a party are you often found:**
a) Huddled in a clique?
b) Talking to someone new?
c) In the kitchen with your best friend?

4. To get others to laugh do you:
a) Tease others mercilessly?
b) Tell jokes?
c) Recount funny anecdotes about yourself?

5. In a room full of people you don't know, do you:
a) Hide in a corner?
b) Find one friendly person and stay glued to them all night?
c) Wander about hoping you don't look alone?

● ●

SCORES
1) a 0   b 5   c 10
2) a 0   b 10   c 5
3) a 0   b 10   c 5
4) a 0   b 5   c 10
5) a 0   b 5   c 10

● ●

RESULTS
0 – 10
Oops! Your social etiquette skills are dismal. While you might find safety with your friends, if you want to appear friendly and open to others you need to move out of your safety zone and allow others in. This means talking to new people, not using others as a means of humor and keeping your body language open and responsive to others.

15 – 30
Your etiquette skills aren't bad but they are hindered by your lack of confidence. You don't have to be what others want you to be, or keep your friends happy no matter what. Instead think about what you want to achieve when you're out, and hold your head high. Use the tips from this book to make new friends and influence people.

35 – 50
Well done, you are an etiquette expert! You not only know how to work a room, but also how to welcome new people in and keep your friends happy. Your communication skills are spot on!

glossary

body language The conscious and unconcious gestures, movements and mannerisms we use to communicate with each other

cluster signals A group of body language signals someone may give you to get their point across. For instance, if they like you they may smile, lean in to you when you speak, mirror your body language and touch your arm when they speak

extrovert A person who is naturally outgoing and confident and has no problems in large groups or asserting themselves in a crowd

flirting A form of body language that expresses a romantic interest in another person. Flirtatious people also know how to use their tone of voice and verbal skills as well as their body language to get their point across

insecure Unsure and in need of confidence

introvert A person who naturally prefers to be alone with his/her thoughts. They are not comfortable in crowds and don't yearn to be the center of attention. Not all introverts are shy – see "shyness"

posture The way you hold your body. Good posture is where your body is relaxed and in natural alignment, whether you're standing, sitting, talking or lying down

shyness Anxiety in social situations that causes a person to feel afraid, nervous and anxious by the thought of talking to someone they don't know or being with people they don't know

small talk Conversation for the sake of conversation i.e. talk about nothing very important. It is a prized social skill

tactile communication Emotion that's expressed to you via touch, i.e. a gentle touch on the arm by someone's hand when you are being consoled

vocal tone The pitch of your voice. This can be used to express authority, nervousness, and confidence without changing what you are saying

further information

Shyness
kidshealth.org/teen/your_mind/emotions/shyness.html
Kids Health is an advice site for teens which includes
tips for overcoming shyness.

www.shykids.com
Tips on how to deal with shyness.

Bullying
www.stopbullyingnow.hrsa.gov/
Contains resources for teens that are bullies and teens who are
the victims of bullies. It explains what bullying is, what teens can
do, and has games and interactive activities.

Body language
changingminds.org/techniques/body/body_language.htm
body language for interviews (not specifically aimed for teens)
www.cnn.com/2006/US/Careers/10/16/cb.fired/index.html

Relationships
www.girlshealth.gov/
GirlsHealth.gov is a website about girls' health.
The relationships section includes information on
parents, siblings, friends, and dating. Quizzes and
interactive images make it fun.

Index

Printed in the U.S.A. — CG